Nursing From The Other Side

"A journey of a brain aneurysm/stroke recovery as a nurse-patient"

By Robyn Schlemmer

DEDICATION

Dedicated to my loving husband, my ever-devoted sons and their wives, my inspiring grandchildren, sisters and brother and my countless, faithful friends who were constantly at my side.

To Lahneen, my forever friend. She fought a good fight and gave me so much support and encouragement. She will always be with me.

A special thank you to my godson, Zack. He passed away in 2012, from an unexpected, sudden illness. He was 16. After much thought and clarity; I realized he helped me wake up. He told me it was not my time and to tell his mom and dad he's okay and that he loves them. He told me to go back home.

About the Author

A wife, mother, grandmother, sister and friend; roles she holds dear to her heart. However, one of her greatest accomplishments and role, is being a nurse of 32 years. Working as a nurse in labor and delivery, post-partum and nursery, brought her many special moments and great satisfaction. But all of this came to halt, with a traumatic brain injury. Surviving, with limitations, she lives the struggles "one day at a time".

To communicate with author, private message or join her group, Nursing from the Other Side, on Facebook

INTRODUCTION

January 23, 2017. A day that will change my life forever. It started as any other, a typical Monday. Work was very hectic; I am a Schedule Coordinator for a very busy obstetrics unit. After work, I went to the gym and got my 12,000 steps in! Losing weight and getting in shape has been a diligent effort, for a couple of months. Leaving the gym in a rush, I head to an acupuncture appointment at 6:00 p.m. It's now 7:00 p.m. I'm back home, we eat dinner and I get things ready for the next day. Then it happened. Suddenly, my head was pounding, and I felt like my neck was broke! A headache like I had never had before.

I laid down, with ice to my neck; I told Jim to just let me rest. At 10:30 p.m., I said, "Something is wrong; take me to the hospital." We go to the Emergency Room. I told Jim to drop me off and where he should park. I walked into the ER and went to registration and told them I was having a terrible headache. That's where time stopped for me. Jim joined me in triage, my blood pressure was greater than 200/100. They immediately take me to a room. The doctor came in and told him I needed a CAT scan of the head; "I think she has a brain aneurysm." Time stood still for Jim. The doctor couldn't believe that I had walked in and that I had called and talked to my sisters on the way. He said it was very unlikely? But everything that was happening seemed unlikely.

Apparently, I was then medicated and heavily sedated. It was confirmed, I have a ruptured anterior communicating artery brain aneurysm. I needed surgery, but I had to go to one of the sister hospitals, which was the Stroke Center. The next few hours were crucial; a bed was not available till early in the a.m. I was transferred to the other hospital and apparently examined by the neurosurgeon and consented to surgery. Jim said I was awake at the time; none of which I remember. It's 8 a.m. on January 24, and I have gone to surgery.

Surgery is over; the aneurysm was coiled, to stop the bleeding. The doctors come out to update Jim. They stopped the bleeding, but towards the end of the procedure an artery went into spasm and blood supply was lost for about 3 minutes. They told Jim that if it is less than 5 minutes, there is usually no complications. Thirty minutes after going to recovery; they called Jim back and told him something was wrong, and they were taking me back to surgery. There was no further bleeding, but I had had a right-sided infarct. A stroke; leaving my left side flaccid.

Apparently, the next two weeks were like a bad dream for me and my family; I struggled with life challenging events. I was intubated, had brain swelling, a blood clot in my right leg and I wouldn't wake up. On February 7, still in neuro intensive care, they took me to surgery and did a tracheostomy and placed a feeding tube. Family and friends apparently remained at my side, constantly. During that time, I had very vivid dreams.

Maybe my dreams involved things I heard? Or was it just all a part of the brain injury?

Now is where my story begins or at least, I think. I am beginning to wake up. This is where I take you on my journey of recovery and nursing from the other side; being a nurse-patient.

** The quotations at the beginning of each chapter were given to me by an amputee, that I knew growing up. She has faced many adversities, but never gave up! She started a text blog and sends out daily quotes of inspiration; I was added to her blog while in the hospital. It was amazing how some days they were exactly what I needed to heart!

"You are not a product of your circumstances.

You are a product of your decisions."

Stephen Covey

CHAPTER 1

I hear voices and alarms. My left arm and leg really hurt; and they won't move. I can't talk. Everything is fuzzy; the TV is on, but I don't understand. Nothing is piecing together. I don't know where I am at or why I am here. None of this makes sense. I finally figure out that I am in a hospital room. But what hospital? What has happened to me? How long have I been like this? So many questions, but now to find the answers.

It is daylight, a nurse comes in. She makes no attempt to tell me what is going on. Then he walks in; the love of my life. That I do know. Jim kisses me and says it's so good to see your eyes open! Have I been asleep for a long time? If only I could tell him I love you, I can't talk. I am so scared, so confused. He sits with me for a while and then says it's time for him to go. The TV is still on, but I can't connect with anything that is on. In my head I thought it was around Christmas, but there are no Christmas movies on.

Hours pass; I feel pain whenever they turn me. I can't move my left side, I try to make sense of all of this. Nothing is coming together. I have so many questions. If I have been asleep for a while, why is someone not explaining what has happened to me? Or even orient me to place and time. I am trapped in my own body. I am screaming but no one can hear me. It is dark now and things seem lonelier and more frightening.

Two therapists come in and they are going to set me up. How hard could that be? They sit me up, after several attempts. I feel like a rag doll being positioned. My head is spinning. I feel like I'm falling. The pain in my low back is excruciating. "Why don't they lay me back down?" You will be fine they say; I don't feel very fine. Finally, they lay me down; I am nauseated and sweating profusely. They tell me they will send the nurse in with something for pain. It is 10:45 p.m.

The pain is no better. I am having severe spasms in my left leg. The nurse in me wants to know what is going on and why is all this happening? Why doesn't the nurse come? I can't reach the call light; I can't talk because of the tracheostomy. I can't move. I need help. It's midnight, the nurse comes in. She is anything but pleasant and she has no pain medicine. I grab her arm in desperation, and she says, "You are going to have to lay still and stop grabbing things! I will be back with your medicine." Really? I still can't reach my call light. I feel like this is hopeless; it is so dark. All I hear are the beats from the monitor and rhythmic breathing (my own ventilator). The only connection I have is the clock on the wall and the window. I keep looking and praying daylight will come soon!

It's after 1 a.m. and finally I get some pain medicine. Now I can sleep. The only problem with that is I dream. I was later told that due to the brain injury and sedation, you can have vivid dreams. When I sleep, I go to places that seem so real. But why am I here? I seem to always be in a group of people and people I know come and go. I think these people may have been at my bedside and my subconscious maybe heard their voices. You react to what goes on around you even if you're asleep, but why does it all seem so real? In my dreams I am okay for a while and then I go back to a room and I am very sick. It must mean something; but what?

The nurse comes back! She is yelling again for me to lay still. She needs to have a little compassion. I don't understand her attitude; none of this is my fault. And isn't her job to care for me? If only I could tell her how mad I am and that if she would just explain what she is doing and be a little empathetic, I just might be a little cooperative.

*NURSING FROM THE OTHER SIDE:

Always listen to your patients, even if they can't talk! Remember they have pain, they may be scared, and they want and need answers. Orient them to time and place often; they need help finding their way through the darkness. It all comes down to basic nursing care. With that being said, the definition of care should be your guide; the provision of what is necessary for the health, welfare and protection of someone you are responsible for.

If you are caring for a patient with a diagnosis you are unfamiliar with; it is in your patient's best interest to learn all you can, to best care for them. How does their condition affect their physical ability? Has their illness or injury affected the way they think or feel? It is your responsibility to look at the whole picture.

Be their guide, their confidant, and always make sure your actions show you are there for them. Make sure that your patient always has their call light; even if they can't or don't use it; you made the effort to show them you would be close by. Even if a patient can't verbally speak; is there actions or body language trying to tell you something and are you responding appropriately. Stop and listen!

"Always leave people better than you found them."

Esther

CHAPTER 2

I have been in ICU for 21 days and they say I must go somewhere else, a different hospital. I don't understand. I hear Jim talking; he doesn't know what to do. He just keeps shaking his head. He must decide where I need to go. I must go to a rehabilitation facility, until I can get off the ventilator at night. Then I can go to the rehab hospital. Why can't I go to a step-down unit here in this hospital? I don't understand. I wish someone would help him; help me.

I had so many questions and no one asked me what I wanted. I have never felt so out of control. Feeling like a rag doll; being positioned and moved like they want. They get me up to the chair again and it wasn't any better. My low back is killing me. The pain is so bad, I can't focus. I am sweating and nauseated; begging to go back to bed. The nurse tells me when she gets some help, she will put me back to bed. It seems there is always an excuse.

I finally get back to bed. It feels like I have run a marathon. I have no energy, no stamina at all. They had to use a Hoyer lift to get me back to bed. I feel like I have been stripped of part of my dignity; I am no longer the nurse in charge. My life has been turned upside down. I lay there, trying to rewind; but I can't get back to where this all started. How did I get to this point? More importantly, how do I get past it?

Jim comes back and says we are leaving, and he will meet me at the facility. I have only been awake for a couple of days and now it's time to go somewhere else. It's like leaving with unfinished business. There are so many unanswered questions. I just wish that anyone that comes in to my room would address me; I want to have a say in what is going on. I want to be stronger; I want this feeling of desperation to be over. It is getting dark outside. The nurse comes in, tells me "good luck" and that the ambulance will be here shortly. I guess that was her version of discharge instructions! I don't know if I am being impatient or they are not adequately doing their job. The nurse in me really wants to be informed. But, for now I guess I just must be the patient. However, I'm not a very willing one.

The ambulance crew arrives and finally someone acknowledges me by name. They tell me they will take good care of me. I nod in agreement. I am transported to the stretcher and strapped in. I truly am a prisoner in my own body. As the ambulance heads to the facility, the surroundings through the window don't look familiar. I thought I was coming from Sarasota to Fort Myers, but in a short time, we are at our destination. I am really confused. These past 3 weeks I have not been where I thought. I have been in Fort Myers this entire time, I was at the hospital I use to work at! So, what has been real or just part of this dark, warped sense of time?

I get placed in a room and transferred to bed. The room is quiet and cold. There is no one there to greet me; no one to tell me where I am at. Jim comes in. So glad he is here! If only I could ask him about where I have been versus where I thought I was. A doctor comes in to assess me and says she will write orders. The entire time, she talks as if I'm not lying right there. She leaves and Jim says it's time for him to go. Are they leaving me in this room? I assumed it was just an admitting area. I'm in pain and little did I know that this would be the beginning of a living "hell" for me.

*NURSING FROM THE OTHER SIDE:

As nurses, never forget to really communicate with your patients. They need to know what you are doing and why. Even if the patient can' t verbally communicate; you can still talk to them. They can still here your explanations and your words of encouragement and reassurance. Your patient needs to know there is someone there for them; take the time to hold their hand and listen, even if there are no words spoken.

. Make sure families are involved in all education and are kept informed; involve them in decision making. If they need assistance, get them with a social worker or case manager. Teach your patients to be assertive with their healthcare concerns. Tell them to ask questions and help them understand what important information they need to know. They need to know you are there to listen. Their families also need to know what questions to ask; help guide them through this journey. Unexpected illnesses or injuries may make it difficult for them to make important decisions. Being a patient and family advocate is just as important as the physical care.

"You don't have to move mountains. Simply fall in love with life.
Be a tornado of happiness, gratitude and acceptance.
You will change the world just by being a warm, kind-hearted human being."

Anita Krizzaz

CHAPTER 3

I wake up, it's dark outside. Jim is sitting in the chair beside me. He looks so tired. He smiles and I know I can do this! He has been and is my strength; our unspoken words mean so much.   Now he says it is time for him to go home. I don't want him to go; I don't want to stay here. He kisses me good night. I want so bad to tell him, "I love you and please, just take me home." I muster up a feeble smile, as he walks out the door.

It's 7:05 p.m. and two nurses come in to give and get report. I am still in the same room. This is where I will be for the night. I am still in a lot of pain. I just wish I knew why I was having so much pain and still not able to move my left side. I try to tell the nurse and she says she is waiting for the doctor to finish the orders. I have been here for 5 hours; how hard can it be? This pain is making me impatient, with a very low tolerance.

I get distracted by an abrupt respiratory therapist, who tells me I must be on the ventilator at night. So, he proceeds to roughly do what he calls tracheostomy care and connects me to the ventilator. I finally realize that was the rhythmic sound I had heard so many days and nights. My own breathing, by the ventilator. I know that the pain and flaccidity and the ventilator must all be related.   If he was what I had to look forward to, I was in trouble. This was an unwelcomed distraction.

The nurse finally returns with medication, so now I can hopefully get some relief. I go to sleep only to be awakened by that respiratory therapist for a breathing treatment, and he informs me I will be receiving them every 4 hours. Lucky me. So, the night goes on. Every time I go to sleep, someone wakes me. Except, when I do need something. I can't find my call light. I can't yell for the nurse. I can't believe this. I see the nurse walk by and I see nurses and techs at the desk. I cannot take this pain anymore. I finally move enough to disconnect the ventilator tubing.

With the alarm blaring, the nurse comes in. I finally get her to know I am in pain and she says she will have to take my vitals, but I must lay still. Easier said than done. She returns and my BP is 180/100; she seems alarmed. What does she think? So now, she gives me something for my blood pressure; I just want pain relief. I look at the clock, it will be daylight soon. After a long night, I know I have a hard road ahead of me.

At least with no voice, I can still pray. Thankfully God always listens. And he can hear me when I'm screaming and knows when I'm scared. If only I could figure out why. Why did this happen or why did it happen to me? I know I must have faith, but it is hard. As I lay there, I remember what my mother always said, "God never gives you more than you can handle". At this point, he must think I am a super-hero!

It is finally daylight, a new day. We can hope for the best. I try to put the night behind me, but the nurse in me won't let it go. Physical therapy comes in and attempt to assess what I can do. It's probably the first time I really see how flaccid my left side is. I look at my toes and fingers, they won't move. They bend my wrist. It really hurts! They want to sit me up.

All I can think about is the last time I was up, and the memory was not reassuring. They proceed to sit me up. There is severe pain in my left arm and shoulder. I want them to stop. I'm sweating and nauseated. They lay me down. It is just as difficult and as painful as sitting up. I need to tell them, "I had a previous frozen left shoulder." But I can't. One of the therapists says he will be back to exercise the legs in the afternoon. I never saw him again that day.

Finally, a bright part of my day. My good friend and her husband are here. Her smile and eyes say a thousand words. She knows what I need, and I don't say a word. She tidies my room, because that's what she does. She fluffs my pillow and asks me what I need. She really cares. This is what I needed. I must be more patient and be thankful for the good things. She brought me a wipe-off board. At last, a way to communicate.

I start asking questions, the pen is going crazy. There are so many pieces to this puzzle. She can answer some of my questions. I must find a way to put these pieces together. She says it's time for her to go and that Jim will be here soon. I am on my own again, so once again I pray.

*NURSING FROM THE OTHER SIDE:

Florence Nightingale pledged in 1893, ". . . to pass my life in purity and to practice my profession faithfully. . . I will do all in my power to maintain and elevate the standard of my profession." Are you as a nurse able to say this is what I do? Have you made a true commitment? Nursing has evolved greatly since Florence Nightingale, but the basic concept and function is the same.

Every day, every shift, every patient deserves your best. If you tell your patient you will come back, then make sure you go back, and in a timely manner. You are working on your patient's schedule and meeting their needs, not your own! It is easy to get caught up in doing the easiest thing, in the shortest amount of time. Whatever a patient needs at the time, is a priority. Make a mind-change of looking at your care from the patient's point of view.

Be accountable for your actions. Never assume you know what your patient needs. It needs to be a collaborative effort; ask the patient. If communication is a deterrent, then find a way to know what your patient needs. Never leave your patient in pain or in distress. They need to know and feel that their comfort is important.

Make sure that the patient's perception is that you love what you do. Your attitude shadows what you do; perception is everything! And yes, the patient is always right, or they should at least think so. Remember, you are their light through the darkness; their hope in tomorrow.

"No beauty shines brighter than that of a good heart."

Anonymous

CHAPTER 4

My days continue to be long. Physical therapy is not real productive.; I am lucky if they even come in to say "Hi". I finally figured out with help from the nurse practitioner, that I was in their Intensive Care Unit. They are going to wean me off the ventilator at night and then I can go to a room on the floor. Now was that so hard? Someone finally explains what they are doing and why. A little reassurance at last, now to get on with it!

One of my nurse confidants is here. She says I look better. I ask her questions about my time in the other ICU. I'm still needing to put the timeline in order. I knew she had been there, but she said she was never my nurse. So that opens more questions, she was in a lot of my dreams. The images of her caring for me seemed so real. I ask more questions; she answers the best she can. She cries and says, "I'm just so glad you are here!" We cry together.

She tells me we need to work on my hair. So, after two attempts with the call light and with no response, she goes to the station to find a comb. How could something so simple be like an impossible scavenger hunt? She returns with a black comb. My hair is a mess. She tries to comb the back; it is matted, a tangled mess. I only remember them using a shampoo cap once, but never anyone combing my hair. She is starting to get through the mattes, but my hair is coming out in clumps. Thank goodness I'm not tender-headed. She does what she can. Whew! That was like a workout. Hating to see her go, she says her good-bye. Now to rest!

I wake up and this is not a dream. Jim is here; just seeing him sitting there, is a comfort. I ask him questions (re: per the wipe-board) about what happened. He begins to sob, and says, "I don't know if I can talk about it. We almost lost you. What would I have done without you?" I hold his hand and we both cry. He gently kisses my cheek; I mouth I love you. We sat there in silence, till it is dark outside. He looks at the clock. I know it's time for him to go. He looks so tired. He tells and kisses me good night. I come up with a feeble smile and he leaves. Another night to face alone.

The nurse coming on is the one from last night, so I'm in good hands, I think. It's 10:00 p.m. and a doctor comes in. He is a gastroenterologist, following up with the abdominal x-ray I had this a.m. Asking me yes and no questions, he then completes an exam. He seems nice enough, I am just not very receptive, I am so tired. He says he will write orders and to have a good night. Well, he ruined the start of it; making rounds at that late hour, is not too conducive to sleep.

About 11:30 p.m., the nurse comes back in and says the doctor ordered an enema, because I am impacted. She continues with the bad news. He wants you to have it tonight! I don't know if I want to cry or scream (if I could) or both. So, at midnight the certified nurse's aide (CNA) and nurse come in and turn me and give the enema. She tells me to call when I need the bedpan. An enema is bad enough on its own; but to be on a ventilator and it is 12:30 p.m., is borderline being ridiculous. So much for letting the patient rest! At this moment, I feel like their perception is, she can't move or talk, so what else does she have to do? Let me think. Oh, yes. SLEEP.

I look at the clock. It is 2 a.m. and the cramping is terrible. I call for the bedpan and the CNA comes in, lifts the sheet and says not yet and leaves. Oh, my goodness! I kept thinking I've got to get through this. I remembered Jim talking about doing an abdominal massage, for cramping. Who would have thought, I can't move my left arm or leg, but I can remember an abdominal massage? I begin rubbing, starting up high on my abdomen working downward. After several times, the cramping lessens. At 3:10 a.m., I once again ask for the bedpan. The CNA returns and sighs and says, "Okay, we will try."

After sitting on the bedpan for almost an hour, the two return. Good job they say. It's my lucky day; not really feeling a sense of accomplishment. They clean me up and give me some pain medicine, maybe now I can rest. However, the rest was short-lived. At 5:15 a.m., they return and say it is time for my bath. You have got to be kidding! We couldn't have done this an hour and a half ago! They finish my bath and change my bed. During the bath I try to go somewhere, trying not think about all that I have lost. It's 6:05 a.m. I will have a whole hour till shift change. I will finally rest, while I can. This has been a lost night.

*NURSING FROM THE OTHER SIDE:

Even though you are busy with your patient's needs, remember, their time is still theirs. Simple things like the timing of procedures or getting ADL's done, can be monumental to a sick patient. What would be the most beneficial and the most reasonable for your patient? If you do have to do a procedure at an odd hour; explain it to your patient. Apologize for the inconvenience and reinforce how it is beneficial to their recovery.

Yes, it may mean consulting with a physician or following up with a care plan. If you do contact a provider, be ready with an alternative plan. But you are there for your patient, not what is easiest or most convenient for you. Again, communicate with your patient as to the what and why of the treatment required. Don't expect them to know, if you have not taken the time to tell them. What your patient thinks is important. Your actions perpetuate their perception.

Be attentive to what your patient and their room look like. Did they have a bath today? Has oral care been done? Do they need their hair combed? Is their bedside table straightened and trash and linens picked up? Take care of your patient like you would your own family member or even yourself. Ask the patient and/or family what their daily routine is. Keeping to their usual routine, will give them some sense of control and normalcy. You'd be amazed at how much better it feels when your hair is combed, and teeth are brushed. How the room is kept, helps families know how their loved one is cared for. This is where it pays to sweat the small stuff!

"Attitude is everything, so pick a good one."

Wayne Dyer

CHAPTER 5

It's the end of the second week here. Days are long and my time is spent thinking and praying. I see the occupational and physical therapists maybe once a day. Jim finally convinces them to start me on steroids for my back pain. I was going to refuse to get up in the chair, but it wasn't offered today. I'm a little confused with the practice here. For being a rehabilitation facility, there is not much rehab occurring. I feel like I am just biding my time; but to do what?

The nurse practitioner comes in and says they will begin weaning off the ventilator at night. That brings on a whole new set of questions. Why do I have a tracheostomy anyway? I know that I can't move my left side; I had a stroke. But, I have so much pain in my left shoulder and spasms in my left leg. The tracheostomy and the pain must be related to the stroke? If only someone would explain. The unknown and the unanswered questions is as frustrating as the pain. I seem to be on vicious cycle, that seems to have no end.

My friend and her husband come. She straightens my bed and tries to comb my hair. She concludes that I really need my hair washed. That would be wonderful. And a shower would be like a dream come true! I haven't seen myself in a mirror for weeks; then again, I'm not sure I want to. Just to have a somewhat normal day, would be amazing. I guess it's true, you don't miss it, till it's gone. Having visitors is such a good distraction.

The day starts to go downhill. I am having severe bladder spasms. I note this on the white board and for my friend to get the nurse. She finds the nurse and says she will be in. Thirty minutes pass and the pains are constant now. I note it as 12 on a scale of 10! I turn on the call light and my friend tell them I am having more pain. They will send in the nurse. Where have I heard that before?

It's now been over an hour; I am crying, my friend is pacing. She goes to the door repeatedly to look for the nurse. One hour and twenty-two minutes since we first called, the nurse comes in. She says, "Honey, what's wrong?" Oh, now she's concerned! I tell her I can't stand the pain and I'm sure I have a UTI. She says she will check the Foley; it is draining but now the urine is red. She says she will talk to the nurse practitioner (NP). Please give me something for pain; I plead, as best I can. She leaves the room. I can't scream; I just cry. My friend looks at me in desperation.

The nurse comes back with a portable US; we need to see if you are retaining urine. I write to her, I must have something for pain first! She sighs and reluctantly goes and gets pain medicine. The US shows no retained urine. She gets a urine sample and sends it to the lab. A few minutes later, the NP comes in. The pain is no better. I tell her I need something for the spasms. She tells me she didn't know I was having spasms; the nurse said I was having some pain. Boy, the communication ball got dropped here. She is also concerned because my heart rate and blood pressure are elevated. No kidding! What did she expect?

After two doses of IV pain medicine, an antispasmodic, and an IV dose of blood pressure medicine, I finally get some relief. The nurse comes in later and says I have a severe urinary tract infection. Who would of thought? She says they will start me on antibiotics right away. I'm a nurse and I know my body, just because I can't move my left side doesn't mean I can't think. I know I'm not stupid. The afternoon has been exhausting and trying.

I close my eyes and try not to think. Sleep does not come, and the events of the day don't stop either. Jim comes in, after he gets off work. That smile fills my heart and gives me hope. He asks, "How was your day?"

*NURSING FROM THE OTHER SIDE:

Today should have never happened the way it did. You must LISTEN to your patients. They should never have undue suffering on your watch. It is not only expected; it is your job! Accurate communication, in a timely manner, must occur between the nurse and the practioner. If you don't think you are getting the response that is best for your patient; then keep asking questions. Persist till you get what the patient needs. Follow your chain of command , if you must.

Should I have had to suffer for over 2 hours? Should I have been made to feel like I was crying needlessly? Pain can be all consuming. It can make a bad situation unbearable. You must address why your patient is having pain, and then it must be a priority to help alleviate it. To a patient, pain can be debilitating and when not relieved, hopelessness sets in. In that moment time stands still and every minute seems eternal. As the patient, you trust that your nurse will take care of you and make decisions in your best interest. As a nurse you were trained to assess your patients and then plan to meet their needs. Sometimes you must think outside the box. Have you tried any non-pharmacological interventions? Heat or ice, repositioning, aromatherapy; just to name a few.

Give your patients your compassion, your time and be committed to do the job you were hired to do. Patient first must be your guide. Consistently reassess what is helping and what is not. Being creative and willing to act, may be the answer. Make sure everyone is on the same page with the patient. The key is communication; with the patient and about the patient. It is called a care plan for a reason. You can make a difference; you can be the catalyst for change. Ask yourself. is this how I would want to be cared for?

"One step can make all the difference."

Anonymous

CHAPTER 6

OMG! I have the best surprise ever. Two of our friends have driven from Missouri to see me. Friends can make all the difference; a pleasant surprise is just what we needed. Jim even seems more at peace and he is smiling! That smile melts my heart; he needs something to smile about. But it gets better, my best friend is coming tomorrow. She knows me like no one else. Her faith, strength and love are a true inspiration. We have been through so many things together; having someone who knows your heart; even when you say nothing at all. It will be a welcome break and diversion for Jim's weekend.

The antibiotics are working. Pain is minimal, and I made it through the weekend! Sunday night I was off the ventilator and vitals remained stable. The NP says I can go to a step-down room, when one is available. It's an uneventful Monday; sometimes boring is good. Yes! I have not been up in the chair, nor does therapy come in regularly. That is one fire, I will let burn. However, I know I am getting weak and I know I must move to get better. I still get confused at times; still trying to piece it all together.

Jim comes in later than usual. He looks very tired. He has had a real busy day at work. I tell him about the plan to move to another room. He reassures me it is a step in the right direction. I trust him, but I'm not convinced. He sits and holds my hand and I know with him beside me, I can do almost anything. We talk about the weekend and how blessed we really are. As much as I hate to; I tell him I probably won't move tonight, so go on home. He agrees and leaves at 8:05 p.m.

I once again sit in the dark and my mind races. But that was short-lived. At 9:30 p.m., two nurses enter and turn on all the lights. One introduces herself as the charge nurse and that I am moving to the other room. After waiting all day and now we move! Why doesn't this surprise me? Once again, a rocky start to another night. The bed I'm in can't go to the other room; so, they transfer me by stretcher to the other bed. Then they realize the air mattress is not on. They use a bed lift to raise me up; and I am left up in the sling, for what seems like an eternity. The air mattress is placed, and I am lowered into bed. At 11:00 p.m., I am finally settled in bed. This was ridiculous! I am in a private room; that had been something I was worried about.

My respiratory therapist (who we will call Mike) comes in. Thank God; someone I know and can trust. He apologizes they moved me so late and did I need anything. I shook my head no. He patted my arm and said it will be okay, "I will check on you often tonight." I sigh in relief. God always gives you light in the darkness. New nurses, new techs; it's frustrating having to adjust to new routines. And it's me that will have to adjust, unfortunately. The night goes by quickly; then again, it was a short night.

As the day starts it is busy in the hallway. There is a nutrition room across the hall, and I must be at the end of the hall because I hear an automatic door open and close constantly. I wonder how it will be different on this unit or will it? My nurse comes in and says my day will consist of physical therapy (PT), occupational therapy (OT), and that a speech therapist will come in to do an evaluation. Let the day begin!

Physical therapy comes in for about 15 minutes and they basically say, because I can't go to the gym, there isn't much they can do. Well, I beg to differ. It feels like every day I continue to get a little weaker. I know now what it means to use it or lose it! Passive exercises could help, but that would require some effort on the part of therapy. The OT comes in and she helps me with a bath; I wash my face and brush my teeth. This has been quite a challenge. I can sit up just briefly, before the spinning and nausea set in. But at least receiving a bath is a start.

At 10:30 a.m., the nurse returns with my morning meds. They were due at 0900. Yes, I watch these things. Who do you suppose watches out for the lay patient? It could be very scary for them. She gives my medications through the PEG tube, and then determines my dressing has not been changed for five days. She smiles and says that somebody wasn't paying attention. I find no humor in her remark. Unfortunately, punctuality and following procedure are not high on the priority list. She changes the dressing and says she will be back to do my bath. She did come back at 3pm!

The speech therapist comes in the afternoon. She does some exercises and I attempt to say some letters. The sound coming out of my mouth seems strange. Not at all like the voice in my head I had never thought about talking being difficult also. She says the doctor will be in tomorrow to view my vocal cords to see if I have any damage. Apparently, the goal is to evaluate the vocal cords and to stay on room air at night. The tracheostomy can then be taken out and I can go to the rehab hospital. At this point, it can't come soon enough.

Friends continue to visit. Collin and his family come to visit; the kids always give me hugs and treat me like nothing has happened. We laugh and cry; my daughter in-law treats me to a pedicure! Bright pink toes make any day better. I talk to Logan and my other grandkids; they talk I listen. Each visit gets me a little more connected with what has gone on. I continue to add pieces to the puzzle.

Nighttime is the hardest. In the quiet and darkness, my mind races and I still go back to those vivid dreams. What do they mean? I am always with a group of people I know, past and present. We are at various places I have been before and some places I have never seen. Trying to hold on, I pray a lot. Thankfully that does not require a voice or a scheduled time. God has given me my life; with some minor adjustments. I will have to find my purpose and my new plan in the scheme of things. Sometimes in the quiet of the night, I wonder if I will ever work again? Will I ever be able to comfort a crying baby or hold a mother's hand? Being a nurse has been one my greatest accomplishments. I love being a nurse.

*NURSING FROM THE OTHER SIDE:

It can't be said enough, "What is best for the patient?" Sometimes common sense needs to be the key player. I think about what I learned in nursing school. What decision would a prudent nurse make in this situation? Again, you must be an advocate for the patient. Transfers should not occur at 10:00 p.m. unless the bed is needed for an emergency. The patient needs to be informed and explanations given, if necessary.

Get to know your patients; they feel like they matter when you take the time to ask. Take the time to read their history; their story may reveal amazing things; well written histories should read like a chronological story. A few minutes of reassurance can go a long way. Sometimes you are the only connection the patient has in their course of care, and each patient is unique in what they need. Knowing what a patient did or their lifestyle, might help you know what they need or expect; even if they can't tell you. Healing of the body goes hand in hand with how the heart feels.

Patients should feel safe, and that they are genuinely cared for. Have patience with their needs. It may seem petty to you, but it may be monumental to that patient in bed. Time is precious to a patient. They have nothing sometimes, but time to think. Ask them how they feel and what they might need to get better. Be considerate and diligent of their time and their needs.

"One of the most powerful things you can do

is take responsibility for your life.

Your choices. Your actions. Your life."

Jeanette Jenkins

CHAPTER 7

The week is progressing. They decide to try and take my Foley catheter out. They will scan my bladder after voiding to check for urinary retention. This makes me a little nervous. But of course, they don't take the catheter out till 6 p.m. I do not understand, why it takes so long to get something done? Is it because if they wait late enough, I won't have to ask for the bedpan? Whatever the reason, I hope for the best. I am to call if I feel the need to urinate.

At 8 p.m. the night nurse comes in. She does a brief assessment and asks if I need the bedpan; I decline. She returns at 10 pm. for my night meds and I ask to use bedpan. The tech comes in; I void a small amount. They do the bladder scan. It is less than 300cc, so they don't have to do anything. I go to sleep for a while. It's about 1 a.m. and I am awakened by severe pain in my bladder. I turn on my call light and through the intercom they ask if they can help me. I can't answer, so they tell me they will send someone in. No one came. I really need to urinate! The pain is getting worse and after 30 minutes, I turn the call light again. The same scenario. They will send someone. What am I going to do? My bladder is full, and the pain is indescribable. After an hour, the tech comes in and says my nurse is responding to an emergency and she will be here as soon as she can. I beg her, as best as I can, to get someone.

I cry in desperation and pain. I wish I could call Jim. I really need him now. The door is open, and I see people going up and down the hallway. I turn on my call light several times; now they just turn it off. I try to find something to throw. I rattle the side rails. Nothing happens. I start yelling "Nurse." It's a struggle to get one word out; even at my best it sounds like a whisper. I see a nurse go by my door three different times, and one time he looked in my door and kept walking. At this moment, I can't take the pain and I truly feel like my bladder could rupture!

I continue to yell, and around 4 a.m. a nurse comes in and says, "Are you calling out?" Yes, I nod. Through my tears, I get her to understand my bladder is full. Seeing I am in pain, she calls for help and scans my bladder. It scans >1000cc. She says she will put the catheter in right now. I thank her repeatedly; the tears won't stop. The catheter is placed. As it is draining, my nurse enters the room and wants to know if there is a problem. It has been 6 hours since she was last in my room and she wants to know if there is a problem?! All I could do was glare at her. But the other nurse says, "Your patient had a full bladder and is in severe pain. You need to get her something for pain right now." She says nothing and leaves to return within minutes with pain medicine. Finally, some relief. They must empty the catheter bag at 1200cc, and it is still draining. Unbelievable!

What a night! An experience I will not soon forget. What if that nurse had not come in? In desperation, I have never felt so isolated, vulnerable, and alone. I truly thought I might die! It starts to get light outside. The more I think about it, the angrier I get. I get pen and paper and begin writing down the sequence of events of the night. After it is written, I read it and cry. This should have never happened. I am so tired, but too agitated to sleep.

When the day nurse comes in, I ask to speak with the charge nurse. The charge nurse comes in a while later. Trembling, I give her the written complaint. I never in my wildest dreams think I would place a complaint against another nurse. But it had to be done.

She reads and apologizes that this happened, not offering much recourse or even excuse, for that matter. I told her that I never wanted that nurse to care for me or be in my room ever! She said she would take care of it. But the damage had already been done.

*NURSING FROM THE OTHER SIDE:

What a learning experience! Unfortunately, it was a perfect example of what not to do. A better approach may have been to do some bladder training before removing the catheter, and to check on your patient more frequently. I may not be able to use my left side, but my knowledge base is still intact. When your patient says something is wrong, LISTEN to them. But, even more, act on it. Ignoring your patients' needs is the same as abandonment.

Granted, there are priorities, but one of them may have been to delegate and report off on any patients that need to be checked or assisted. The tech that came in and said my nurse was in an emergency, should have done more. She should have gone to the charge nurse or another nurse to get help. Never leave your patient in distress. The big picture must be looked at; every patient must be taken care of, appropriately. Your patient is trusting you to "do no harm". Do not leave your patient helpless, feeling hopeless, and without a means to communicate. The nurse that did come in, did as she should; unlike the nurse who completely ignored the situation. Be the nurse who hears a cry for help and responds!

"Negativity is the disease; positivity is the cure."

Anonymous

CHAPTER 8

After last night, I am not sure what the day will bring. But I do know I need to get out of here. At this point, my life depends on it. I will do everything I can to make those that care for me accountable. I have a new appreciation for "sleeping with one eye open". Friends come to visit today; a much-needed diversion. Some are co-workers and they all say how good I look. I don't know what they were expecting, but I guess when you were in a coma for three weeks and had a near death experience, just being awake would seem amazing.

They decide not to take the Foley out for a while. I think that is a good idea. It's either just a good day or coincidental, but my medications were all on time and my call light was answered promptly. Why is it bad things must happen, and complaints made for someone to do their job? (And for the record, when Jim found out about the incident last night, he went straight to the charge nurse, and apparently this was for the second time.) In the quiet, of the afternoon, I once again relive the nightmare of last night. I cry and thank God for being with me.

My day ends with a visit from a good nurse friend. She comes with gifts, but that is just who she is. She brought me a soft coral-colored blanket. It was nice to have something special.; something to bring warmth and comfort to a cold room. I listen, she talks. After she is gone, I lay there in the quiet and darkness and think about what has happened over the last five weeks. They better get ready, because when I can finally talk, I have the questions ready to fire. What will the next five weeks bring? I want all the details and my questions answered.

My memories I do have are sketchy and I don't know what is real and what really happened. It's like being a puppet and someone else is in control. I've had a brain aneurysm, a stroke, a ventilator, a tracheostomy, a blood clot, a feeding tube placed, and then all the unfortunate incidences as a patient. Okay, so no wonder my mind races in the quiet of the night. I think about patients who have no medical knowledge or family to help. What is happening to them? Who is looking out for their well-being? I decide, accountability is what's going to get me through this. I must make sure that those that care for me are accountable for their actions. This will be a challenge, even for me.

Over the next few days the "physical therapy" is about the same. I'm done getting frustrated about the lack of therapy. It is what it isn't. On the other hand, the speech therapy is progressing. They have viewed my vocal cords; there was no damage, and I have movement in the cords. They work every day on trying to say different sounds. It is mentally and physically exhausting. But, by Friday, if all goes as expected; the trach will be taken out. I pray the next two days are without incident. I know that's a lot to hope for

As a nurse patient, you notice the little things and you sweat the small stuff. It's true that when one of your senses is disrupted, the others take over. When you can't talk and your mobility impaired, I think people assume your ears are broke also. People come in the room and have conversations with each other, like you are not there. They talk about other patients, their co-workers and even their relationships or lack thereof! You want to scream, "I can hear you, stupid; and have you heard of HIPPA?" My sense of small is heightened also. Sweet or fruity smells seem to be soothing.

My days remain long, filled with breathing treatments, tube feedings, and medications. I feel like I'm in a time warp; living the same day over and over. I am not improving, but thankfully not getting any worse. It has not been at all what I thought a rehabilitation facility would be. I had hoped to get a head start in getting stronger, but that hasn't happened. But then again, I never thought the simplest of things would be so difficult. Sitting up and turning in bed seem almost impossible; I can't imagine what standing and walking will be like! Or will it happen at all?

The discharge planner has been in gathering information for my impending transfer. The receiving hospital apparently must review my chart and then accept me as a patient. She comes back about three times and says each time, "Oh, I forgot. I need to ask you one more thing." Since I can't communicate, except through the whiteboard; shouldn't Jim be here to answer some of these questions? What if that facility won't accept me, then what? There are too many what ifs or maybe I am just a little nervous and apprehensive.

*NURSING FROM THE OTHER SIDE:

Have you done everything you could for your patient today? That doesn't mean you will fix everything or cure them. It means you have worked to best of your ability and in your patient's best interest. Did you make them feel important and that they mattered? If you answered yes, job well done. But if it was a hesitant no, we have some work to do! Start every shift ready to learn something new and how you can make someone's day better. Looking for the positive takes a lot less effort than dwelling in the negative.

Your patient's needs must be a priority. They need to know that you are there to keep them safe. It's not that hard., Nursing 101; basic nursing care. To best take care of your patient, you must be a continued presence; to know what your patient needs. Again, talk with them and listen, both to verbal and boy language. Those extra few minutes you spend with them can make all the difference. Sometimes just being present is all they need.

Remember as a child the song "Oh Be Careful"? Be careful little tongue what you say. Be respectful with how you address your patient. Refrain from Sweetie, Honey or Baby. How you address them should be respectful. It's okay to converse with your co-worker. But is what you are saying appropriate for the patient to hear? Including them in the conversation; is a good time to learn about your patient; their likes, dislikes, hopes and fears.

Also, remember to respect your patient's privacy. Be diligent about closing a door or pulling a curtain. Preserving their dignity during any procedure is a must. Patients remember everything you don't do or do wrong, but they also will acknowledge all the little things you do to take care of them. Time may be limited, but a patient should never feel rushed.

Patients and their families or caregivers need to be included in discharge planning. Knowing what the lifestyle and home features include; may better guide the discharge process. If the patient condition warrants, and/or if the patient requests; plan for family to be there. Decreasing the stress for the patient and having as complete information as possible can possibly be achieved with including the family or caregiver.

"There are plenty of difficult obstacles in your path.
Don't allow yourself to become one of them."

Ralph Marston

CHAPTER 9

It's Friday and today is the day. The respiratory therapist comes in (thank goodness it's the one I like…and trust). I get a breathing treatment and then he says he will be back to remove the trach. My heart is pounding. This is scary and wonderful, all at the same time. In a few hours, I will hopefully be able to start asking all those questions and be able to tell my best friend, "I love you." I say a prayer for God to be with me and the therapist. Praying is the one positive I must hold on to.

The therapist comes in and he prepares to decannulate (remove the tracheostomy). He explains that it will hurt a little bit. He must have seen the fear in my eyes, because he pats my arm and quietly says, "It will be okay. Here it goes." He proceeds to remove the trach; it really hurts. He stops a minute for me to relax. There is scar tissue, making it more difficult. He tells me to take a deep breath, and as I do, he twists and pulls hard. The tracheostomy is out! With tears in my eyes, he says can you try and speak. I say, "Thank you." He smiles and nods for a job well done.

Hearing my own voice was kind of surreal. When the therapist leaves, I continue to talk out loud to myself. I had heard it in my head a thousand times before. But today, it was like hearing it for the first time. My nurse comes in and checks the pressure dressing and says that my transfer is complete. I will go to the rehabilitation hospital later today. It is turning out to be a wonderful day! Two hours after the trach was removed my oxygen saturation is staying greater than 95% and I'm not short of breath.

Then it happens; Jim, the love of my life, comes in. He bursts into smiles when he sees the trach is out. I smile and say, "I love you." He cries. We pray together and thank God for getting us this far and keeping us together. I tell him I will be transferred later today; they are arranging the ambulance now. I ask for his phone. I don't know who I want to call first. I call my sons. They both are very surprised and so thankful. My youngest son says who is this, when I say hello. They have tears of happiness. And yes, Jim cries again. The men in my life have gotten so sappy! I continue to make calls. When I call my little sister, she is driving home from work. She is so elated, she must pull off the highway to compose herself. I call my best friends. It is so good to be able to talk to them again. Life's little miracles are the best!

It has been quite a day. But now I need to rest. As I lay there, I began to get nervous about going to the rehab hospital. Don't get me wrong, I'm ready to get out of this place. It's just a new place, new challenges, new routines. The nurse part of me is a creature of habit. It gets to be 5 p.m. and no one has given us an update. Jim takes the last of my things to the car. I ring for the nurse; the intercom comes on. I so intently want to tell them what I think about their call system, but I refrain and ask about what time I will be leaving. The nurse comes in and says the ambulance will be here around 6 p.m. She said all your paperwork is done, right? I hope so in reply. I think this is something she should know.

At 6:05 p.m., the ambulance driver arrives. He verifies my identity and where I am going. I received pain medicine earlier, so hopefully the ride goes well. They secure me on the stretcher. Jim kisses me goodbye and will meet me there. The ambulance is hot, and I am nauseated. And it doesn't help I'm riding backwards. I try taking some deep breaths. I don't want to be sick. I close my eyes, and a few minutes later we are pulling into the ambulance bay. Now to start the next chapter; finally, this nightmare ends.

*NURSING FROM THE OTHER SIDE:

Be empathetic of what your patient is going through. Illness can cause a patient to sometimes act out of character. Their demands or whining may be acting out from pain or fear. They may just need to be reassured or explained what is happening. Remember, that small victories to a patient can be monumental. Take the time to celebrate the victory with them. Again, taking the time to listen will benefit you in the long run. A patient that is informed and is felt truly cared for will be less demanding and more cooperative.

Pay attention to details. In the event of a discharge or transfer, make yourself aware of what has been done or needs to be done. Even if there is a discharge planner, it is your responsibility as the nurse to make sure that everything is completed and that your patient and family is well informed. Are all their questions answered and all their requests taken care of? Also remember that time is endless to a patient. So, do everything in your power to make things happen when they are supposed to. A patient doesn't want excuses, they want your commitment and actions that are perceived as patient centered. When a patient sees you enter the room, all they should feel is contentment and trust; they know they will be taken care of. Are you that nurse?

"One day at a time."

Jim

CHAPTER 10

It is dark outside, and it is close to shift change. A nurse is waiting, when I arrive in the room. This is already a step in the right direction. The nurse asks me questions for admission. It's amazing to be able to answer the questions, out loud. Such an accomplishment to be able to do it all by myself! She couldn't believe that I was talking so well, after just being decannulated that morning. I tell her I have been through a lot to get here; a tear rolls down my face.

She acknowledges that I am a nurse and wants to know how long. I have been a nurse for 32 years, I tell her; 29 years in mother-baby. What I did and know seemed to matter to her. This transition is much easier and I'm so glad I am here. I have a roommate. This is different, but it might be nice to have someone to talk to, now that I can. It is change of shift; the nurse and aide for the night come in. They get report and ask if there is anything I need or want to add. Patient centered care; now this is a new concept and I like it. For sake of privacy, I will call the RN, Ruth, and the aide, Jane. The two of them will soon become my night angels!

The first night is busy, with them trying to complete the admission details and me trying to figure out their routine. Ruth comes in and says she needs to change all my dressings. She apologizes for the late hour, but her genuine concern is reassuring. I let her know it's okay. She changes the IV dressing, the trach site, which she says there is only a small opening. She removes the dressing on the G-tube; it is red and swollen. I can't remember the last time it was changed. Jane comes in and wants to know if I need anything. I am beginning to put trust back in nursing. I am medicated and sleep soundly, no unwanted dreaming.

At last rounds, Ruth tells me that therapy will be coming in this morning for an evaluation and to help me with my bath. And just as she says it, an occupational and physical therapist come in. It's Saturday morning; they evaluate what I can do, but more so, what I can't do. They ask me about the therapy I had at the other facility. I tell them, unfortunately there wasn't much to say. They reassure me it is okay; we will start from here. I basically have lost the last three weeks. So, from here I begin. After their evaluation they sit me on the side of the bed. It was like before, I feel like I'm falling. I keep falling to the left. I can't seem to get my balance. The therapists tell me this is normal and to be expected. They complete my bath and help me dress. Wow! Real clothes. For the first time in a while my butt isn't hanging out! They are done and I am exhausted. I lay back down, and they tell me that my therapists will be in Monday, twice a day. They leave, and as I lay there, I realize I have a long way to go and a lot of hard work ahead of me. It's times like this I still wonder, Why?

I rest for a while. A bubbly, energetic girl comes in my room. She introduces herself as my speech therapist. I will call her Cory. She has me do several facial exercises and repeat several words. It feels strange to make the sounds. "Do you need anything?" she asks. I ask her when I can have something to drink. She explains they need to evaluate my swallowing ability first. But she thinks I'm doing very well. She leaves for a minute and returns with ice chips. I can have a few while she is here. She puts a spoon of ice in my mouth; the cold and the melting ice is amazing. It has literally been weeks since I have had anything by mouth. A tear runs down my face and I tell her "thank you."

Jim comes in the afternoon. He looks more rested than I have seen him for a while. He smiles and says he is glad to see me. I say hello and he grins again and says, "I love hearing your voice!" He tells me he slept better, knowing I was safe. And that he was right about. We talked about my busy day and the thrill of getting ice chips! It is amazing the little things we all take for granted. We both agree that the three weeks at the other facility was a total waste of time as far as therapy went.

After my evaluations today, I came to some frank realizations. I did not realize how bad I was; I have some real physical deficits. It was almost overwhelming and scary, to say the least. I ask Jim if I will get better; will I ever get to work as a nurse again? We sit in silence for a while. He finally says, "You had a severe brain injury that has left you with challenging obstacles to overcome." Wow, that is the first time I've heard severe brain injury. It is hard to hear, but it puts a lot of things into perspective. I realize it is going to take more than time, to heal

But where do we start? He tells me, that's why you are here. They will work with you every day. This is what they are trained to do. It's going to be a lot of hard work. He tells me that I am going to have to relearn how to do many things. My brain doesn't remember how to make my arm and leg move. But I can remember my debit card number and security code. How crazy is that? He holds my hand and with that "special" look he gives, he tells me we will take it "one day at a time." That will be our new mantra.

*NURSING FROM THE OTHER SIDE:

Kindness is amazing. It will come back to you tenfold. Positive thinking with action follow-through is powerful attributes. When a patient feels cared for and that you are genuinely concerned for them, they will be more cooperative and less demanding. Timeliness to patient needs speaks a thousand words. It lets your patient know how organized you are and that they are a priority.

Time management can be one of the hardest things to master. But when it is mastered, your workflow and your attitude will improve. This becomes a trickle effect, because your patient will also reap the benefits. Time management is easier for some than others. But if done efficiently, can be the game breaker for a great shift versus the worst shift ever. It can not only be used at work, but in your home life too. I feel there are three basic concepts to time management:

1. Prioritize. What must be done versus what you would like to get done. The priority may be different for each patient. The patient's support system is also your priority.

2. Avoid unnecessary steps. Combine tasks and gather all supplies needed before you enter your patient's room. Can you do your assessment at medication time? Does the patient need a snack? Call your patient and ask if they need anything before you come.

Gathering all your supplies needed will not only save steps but give you more time at the bedside.

3. Take advantage of downtime. It can be a lot easier to visit with your co-worker, but don't give into that temptation if there is something left to do.

Look at your own game plan (aka your brain list). What are your patients going to need next and when? Is your documentation up-to-date? Have you peed yet? (This must be a priority.) So, in a nutshell, get all your work done, then socialize. It is time to get work ethics in order.

Remember, the patient is first, what the patient needs is second, what the patient thinks they need is third, etc. Get the picture: PATIENT FIRST!

"A sense of purpose is an incredible alarm clock."

Mel Robbins

CHAPTER 11

It's Monday morning, let the fun begin! I have just been introduced to my personal whiteboard. It has my information, my schedule for the day and goals. The best thing is, that it is updated daily and as things change. What a way to communicate and to involve the patient! I'm dressed and ready for therapy. At 7:30 a.m., Cory my speech therapist, comes in. Yes, with more ice chips! We do more exercises and I swallow without difficulty. She says she wants to try something different. She returns with vanilla yogurt. I take a spoonful and I swallow without difficulty. It's as good as having a steak dinner! Cory says she will schedule me for a swallow study, ASAP; but in the meantime, I can only have ice when she or the nurse are present. I have no problem with that.

At the scheduled time, my occupational and physical therapists arrive and introduce themselves. I will call them Willa, my OT, and Kerri, my PT. They explain to me the plan of care and they will communicate to nursing through the whiteboard. It's reassuring that the same therapists will follow me each day. My tennis shoes are put on; the first time for shoes in about seven weeks. I am assisted to a wheelchair that has my name and room number on it. Never did I think I would have a label like this. To think, having to be assisted to a wheelchair and being taken to a gym to learn how to sit up, is almost mind boggling. This brain injury has taken away my career, my livelihood; the life I had is no more. Okay, no time for a pity party! Let's get on with it!

We go to the gym and I am transferred to a treatment table. I'm sweating, dizzy, and a little nauseated. At this point I'm a little scared, frustrated, and vulnerable. The therapists notice I'm pale and encourage me to take a deep breath, relax, and reassure me this is normal, because I have basically been flat on my back for the last seven weeks and my body is trying to adjust being upright. We work on trying just to sit upright and balance. I never thought this would be so challenging. They have me do some reaching exercises to activate unused muscles. My left shoulder is killing me; the motion is very restricted. They work on evaluating what I can do, but to me it's like evaluating everything I can't do.

They take me back to my room. Kerri transfers me back to bed with moderate assistance. I'm exhausted. I call and get something for pain. Now to rest. As I drift off, I'm not sure if I am excited about what I did or overwhelmed as to what I need to do. Maybe a little bit of both. The one thing I do know is that I have a long road and a lot of hard work ahead of me. I go for the afternoon therapy session. I do more of the same, as earlier. It's hard to believe I get tired so easily; my endurance is not much.

I finish the session and go back to my room. They get me back to bed and tell me we will do it all again tomorrow. I think there will be a lot of tomorrows, having agendas out of my control. And as a nurse, I am driven to be in control. But it is very reassuring to know I have trained and knowledgeable therapists helping me. Their concern is genuine; I believe they will become good confidants.

That evening my rehab doctor and physician assistant come in for an assessment. They review my medications and they will work on getting me to medication by mouth. This is the first time someone has explained why I am on the medications I am and what to expect, since I had the aneurysm and stroke. It explains the increased muscle tone, the fatigue, and the emotional roller coaster. They ask if I need anything. Boy is that a loaded question. What I need, they can't give. I tell them no. They will see me daily. The doctor has an almost arrogant way about him; very matter of fact. From my experience, he seems the type to listen but not hear a thing. We shall see.

*NURSING FROM THE OTHER SIDE:

Commitment, prompt response, compassion, and professionalism, all yield to a patient feeling safe, cared for, and trusting those that care for them. It's amazing what a little time and doing your job can make. Positivity promotes faster healing and increased cooperativeness with your patient.

It comes down to the simplest of things:

1. Listen to your patient.

2. Make your presence known.

3. Prompt response to patient needs.

Maybe it would be beneficial for you to reread your job description. If you are not doing everything 100% of the time, you have some work to do. You can always do better.

Always remember you are an advocate for your patient; you may have to be their voice, their link to their doctor. They and their families may need to be educated as to what questions to ask; they need to learn to be pro-active with their healthcare. Every encounter with a patient and their family is a teachable moment.

10 Things that Require Zero Talent (Anonymous)

1. Being on time
2. Work ethic
3. Effort
4. Body language
5. Energy
6. Passion
7. Doing extra
8. Being prepared
9. Being coachable
10. ATTITUDE

"No one is coming to make your life successful.

This life of yours is 100% your responsibility."

Anonymous

CHAPTER 12

Therapy continues to improve; every day is a challenge and I am hanging in there. Once I was able to sit up on my own; I continued with the reaching exercise. I think I could get sick of moving clothes pins from let to right. But I won't give up! It's the complications that get in my way. They are having trouble getting my medications regulated for my increase tone. To get where I need to be, I can hardly keep my eyes open. I guess it is a work in progress. I begin reading everything I can about brain injury and stroke. Neuroplasticity is a recurring theme. It is the means of rewiring the brain, through repetition; hence the clothes pins.

I am having my swallow test today. Cory, my speech therapist, asks what the first thing is I would like to have. I would love to have a Diet Pepsi! I'm transported to radiology; the test is performed by a radiologist and a speech therapist. I swallow various consistencies and they watch me swallow with each by radioscopy. The testing was thin liquids to solid food. I was able to swallow everything, with only mild reflux noted. I must take small sips or bites. I can live with that!

I return to my room. I'm very excited and exhausted at the same time. Cory comes to my room, a short time later, with a Diet Pepsi in hand. Hooray! I take a drink, it is sweet memory of the past. It tastes so good! She says they will start with pureed food; to make sure there are no problems. When you haven't eaten in weeks, even pureed sounds wonderful. The best thing is that by Monday, March 13, my birthday, I can have the Olive Garden; Jim promised me!

My birthday comes and the day starts out amazingly. It's 9 a.m. and I have had birthday calls from Jim, Collin, Logan and my granddaughter. I start receiving flowers. They are beautiful and are coming two or three at a time every hour. My family and friends have overwhelmed me with their best wishes and generosity. But one of the best birthday gifts, I am about to get. Willa, my OT, comes in and asks if I'm ready. I nod. I get a shower today! I have not had a shower since the morning of my aneurysm, January 23. They transfer me to the toilet and taking care of business, has never been more fun! I then transfer to a shower chair and into the shower. Appreciation for running water has taken on a whole new meaning. I shower and wash my hair. With only use of my right arm and hand, I realize that this too is going to be a challenge. Taking a shower will take some thought and preparation. No more quick showers, I guess. We finish and I get dressed and back to bed. My good friend arrives about the time I get back to bed. She is here to dry my hair. To be pampered is great. This is a great start to my 57th birthday!

Jim comes with food from Olive Garden; this is a reward I have worked hard for. It is so nice to be able to share a meal with him. I have missed that time with him. We talk about my day; filled with so many blessings and beautiful flowers! My room looks like a flower garden in full bloom. He holds my hand and cries; he is just so glad I'm here. I have never seen him so emotional. I am still trying to comprehend all he has gone through. Unfortunately, the day has come to an end and Jim must go home. Besides him leaving, the time I dread comes: the darkness and its loneliness.

When the lights go off, the thoughts go rampant. The vividness of the dreams, when I do sleep; awaken me with even more uneasiness. I still have questions about how I got to this point. I lay awake for a long time; I pray. God always listens. Now if he would just give me answers. I know I need be more patient. I am still awake, when the nurse makes rounds at midnight. She tells me something I'm not sure I'm ready to hear. Tomorrow they are going to take my Foley catheter out...again. It makes me kind of nervous. The last time was anything but pleasant. At least this time, I can speak. If I scream, someone will hear me!

I sleep very little that night. In early a.m., they remove the catheter and I am to call when I need to urinate. They will be doing bladder scans after each void. About 9 a.m., I ask for the bedpan. I can urinate, and the scan shows 150 cc of residual urine. I'm off to a good start! It is short-lived, however. About 1 p.m., my bladder is feeling full. I am placed on the bedpan but am unable to void. The bladder scan shows 500cc of urine in my bladder and an in and out catheter is placed to drain my bladder. In the evening, the same thing occurs, and the residual is 600cc this time. I am having bladder spasms. They consult with the physician assistant; the Foley catheter is replaced. It is okay. At least they recognized it wasn't time yet.

A couple of days later I am having bladder spasms and feeling like I need to void. I'm pretty sure I have a urinary tract infection. Therapy does not go well, due to the pain. I tell the doctor, when he makes his rounds. He says your urine is clear. I don't think you have a UTI. I persist and he says if it will make me feel better, he will order a urinalysis. Well, it will make me feel better, but once again, he needs to listen to his patients. The nurse comes in a few hours later and what do you know…. I have a UTI and antibiotics are started. I also learn that any type of infection will affect my spasticity; so, they must increase my medication. It helps, but now I can hardly stay awake during therapy. We are on the roller coaster again.

*NURSING FROM THE OTHER SIDE:

Celebrate your patient's victories and their "special" days. Remember, it's the little things that matter. You can make the difference between a patient having a good day and a day gone wrong. The accomplishments are more meaningful, when they are recognized by others.

It still comes down to spending time with your patient and giving them the "why" and "how" of what you are doing. That time spent with your patient could be the simplest, yet the most valuable thing you can do. A patient's acknowledgement of what to expect increases their positive perception of their expectations. Remember, the patient's perception is not only based on what you do, but also what is not done.

Being a patient advocate must be a priority. It may mean you have to be assertive and help the patient to get the doctor to listen. Never put the physician on the defensive, rather communicate in reference to him as, "Your patient needs or requests…".

The physician may not care what the nurse thinks, but he will never want to look bad in front of his patient. Remember, you can be the light in the darkness.

"When writing the story of your life,

don't let anyone else hold the pen."

Anonymous

EPILOGUE

It's not ironic that I end this writing on Chapter 13. It's my lucky number and fate has brought me here. I will summarize how my rehabilitation progressed and fast forward to where I am now. I proceeded with daily occupational and physical therapy, working towards being able to function at home. I work on sit/stands, transfers, and I even am taking a few steps with moderate assist. Everything is revolved around repetition; the neuroplasticity. My Foley catheter is finally removed, and I am voiding without difficulty. Satisfactorily eating mechanical soft food, my feeding tube is removed, and I am officially tube free. My speech and swallowing continue to improve with daily exercises. Unfortunately, my taste buds are a little askew. Sweets taste the best. I will have to be careful with that. But for now, I think I have earned the right to have daily ice cream!

By week 10 of my short-term disability (I have 12 weeks of short-term payments), I receive my first payment. The whole process was ridiculous and required too much unnecessary stress. But that is a whole different discussion. Long story short, the day I got my first short-term payment, I had to submit paperwork for my long-term disability. The support I got from human resources was less than helpful. On the bright side, the support from family and friends has been most overwhelming. My co-workers, past and present, donated their paid time-off hours to me; the amount was amazing; they really took care of me. When I was notified, I sobbed. I couldn't believe it. But Jim and my sons said, "Mom, you made a difference!" This is one of the best shows of selflessness I had ever seen; they too have made a difference. These amazing co-workers are all my "Baby Angels."

I also received many cards, gifts, and flowers from near and far. I heard from people I hadn't seen in years. This is one of those times that social media did a good thing. Collin and Logan told me to go to their pages and look back, starting with the day of my brain injury. Oh, my goodness! They had posted daily what was going on and there were hundreds of responses; posts giving encouragement, support, and prayers. With the posts I was able to put some of the pieces together; the timeline was finally making sense. Thankfully there were people there for my family, when I couldn't be.

After 96 days (week #15) in the hospital, I came home. Not functioning as independently as I like, but at least I am home. It has been frustrating. It seems like everything is a challenge. From the doorways not being wide enough for the wheelchair, to not being able to get dressed by myself. I am adjusting, some days more willingly than others. I really miss cooking and even doing laundry; I can help, but it is just not the same. You also don't realize how much independence you lose, when you must rely on someone else for just about everything. No more impromptu shopping trips!

Fast forward, it's now been one year since my brain aneurysm. I still have limited use of my left arm and leg; have moderate to severe muscle spasms with increased tone which affects my balance and my ability to transfer and walk. I am going to therapy two days a week, doing a home therapy program two to three days a week, and have gained new knowledge and appreciation of the use of essential oils. They have been useful with relaxation, sleep and several physical ailments. I have a caregiver for part of the day, for safety. That being the key; you do what you must to be safe.

On July 9, 2017, I was released as an employee of the hospital system. That was a day I never thought would come; not being a nurse. A nurse is all I ever wanted to be. God gave me not only an amazing career, but a feeling of great accomplishment! I am proud to say that I was good at what I did and have made a difference. In August, I was given full disability. Not sure it was a gift I really wanted, but it is all I can do to help Jim for now. I continue to get great and continuous support from family and friends. I will forever be grateful.

All bad things do have a silver lining. This tragedy has brought my brother back to me. It is beyond words what a relationship with him again means. He showed up at the hospital while I was still in a coma; Jim was elated and comforted. When they told him, I might not make it; they called the family in. My mom had made me promise, before she passed, that I would do everything to keep the family together. Somehow, I don't think she meant to this extreme! And my wonderful sisters have been there every step of the way! We have always been close, and I really need them now. Family means everything, in times like these.

Collin and Logan and their wives have been such a comfort to Jim and me. Being right there for their dad, even though at times it was trying.

The day they told Jim I might not make it; Logan let the doctors know what he thought (in not so many words!). My grandchildren have been and continue to be my cheerleaders, I am still just Mama, with some minor adjustments. They never give up on me.

But, my gratitude to Jim is insurmountable. He has been and is truly amazing. He is patient (well, most of the time), kind, always forgiving and always there to cheer me on or pick me up when I fail. Over 30 years ago, we made a promise, for better or worse, and this whole process has taken its toll. But we work together; facing every obstacle and celebrating every victory; united. Yes, this is what love is . . .; he is the love of my life.

This journey has taught me many things. Having faith in God and trusting in his strength, has gotten me through many difficult days. Praying was always a way for me to communicate; voice or not. Learning after I woke up; how many prayer chains and prayers were given for me; that was faith affirming. I have learned to be humbler; never taking anything for granted. We are not given any guarantees in life; so, every effort needs to be made to see the good in everyday and live like there was no tomorrow. Hope only works, when it lives in the heart.

Always ask questions; never leave anything to chance. After being a patient, in the worst of circumstances, you must stand up for yourself. If you can't, then your family must be your advocate. If it is not right for you then say no, but don't stop there. Every survivor, every patient is unique, as is the process to recovery. Every decision needs to fit your needs and functionality. You must start by realizing you may not function as you use to. Self-realization and adaptation can be a very large pill to swallow.

I have had to give up a lot, but God left me here for some purpose. With my cognitive ability still intact, I think somedays, my purpose is just to keep things running smoothly! I will work daily to find my new purpose. Finding my new normal is an ongoing process. Having had a traumatic brain injury (TBI), my physical and emotional health is like being on a roller coaster. Your emotional responses may seem inappropriate sometimes; but not intentionally. After much research, I have found that everything is affected by a TBI; it depends on what part of the brain has been affected (A good question to be asking). Simple infections like a urinary tract infection or sinusitis, affect my spasticity (muscle tone); making it worse, thus making it more difficult to ambulate and with increase pain. So, nothing is simple. Fatigue is also a big trigger of untoward symptoms, sleep is away for the brain to heal. You confront each obstacle head on; and remember that there may be two steps back, for one step forward. What matters is that you do move forward.

Opportunities for improvement and support are available. But you must look for them. I take advantage of my cognitive abilities; reading and research is very rewarding. Also journaling, can bring clarity and open new doors; such as writing a book! Join a support group or be a part of an online blog. I have joined a brain aneurysm and a stroke survivor online support group and its nice to share with others having the same experiences as you. There is strength in numbers and learning is healing.

I continue to research all the effects of a traumatic brain injury. Your brain, I have learned, is very integral in your emotional and physical health. And, yes you can rewire your brain. Through a process of neuroplasticity, use of repetitive exercises, you reteach the brain what to do. But why all the sleepless nights and mood swings? Part of my confusion was reversed, and clarity came when I read the following article. Finally, an understanding, for the way I felt and the experiences I am having: It sometimes takes validation for us to be able to understand and accept that which has caused us harm.

Having a Brain Injury (it never ends…)

by Linda W. Arms, June 22, 2014

What is a brain injury like? It's not like a broken leg. It's not like most other medical conditions or diseases. It's not getting old and experiencing "senior moments". It is very different although many people look at it as "oh, you'll get over it" or "I have that too, it's what happens when you age."

A brain injury, whether from trauma, stroke, aneurysm, lack of oxygen or other cause, happens quite suddenly – out of the blue.

You are fine; everything works; your mind is active and full of ideas and dreams and thoughts; you walk about without a problem. You can speak and comprehend what someone is saying while you cook or do something else. You read, watch TV, drive, cook, solve problems, make decisions.... Most likely you don't think about your brain at all, but it is what is making those things all possible.

After a brain injury, you suddenly are unable to move about or think like you did before. Brain injuries vary in their effect on a person depending on the severity and which parts of the brain were damaged. In many cases after a significant brain injury, your mind is blank without any thoughts unless you force them to be there. You have to concentrate on thinking through a simple thing in your head because you lose your focus very easily. You are in a fog. When you try to think through a simple thing you feel like your head is full of thick mud or dense cotton that muffles and gets in the way of thinking clearly. Sometimes it's impossible to think even about the simplest thing, the blankness just returns.

There is a sense of other worldliness around you. Your senses are muffled. Your sense of presence is gone. You feel you are not really part of what is happening around you. You can't experience everything going on around you. Your view into the world around you is very small like looking through a little tube. Your awareness is missing. You often just stare off into space with emptiness in your head and in your eyes.

You have problems understanding what people are saying to you. You have problems talking and explaining something you want to say. You can't find the words, the words don't come out right, and sentences are hard to form. You have few emotions, there is no joy, there is no happiness, there is no anger, there is no sentimentality, there is little except maybe some sadness and nothingness.

You have to hide in a safe, quiet place because the world is too chaotic for you. You can't go to stores, you can't hear sounds, you can't have too much movement around you before you feel so overwhelmed, you can't see straight or walk right. You have to move slowly because you don't have the strength or energy, you have to be careful walking through doorways or passing by things because things aren't really where you see them to be. You have odd sensations in your head, you have odd tingling in parts of your body, you may not feel pain the way you used to.

You're cold all the time, it's hard to get up out of a chair or out of bed because you are so weak. You are tired, always tired. You sleep and sleep for sometimes 14 – 16 hours a day. You get up in the mornings and it takes hours to feel alert enough to function. You sit there waiting for the disturbing sensations in your head to settle down while your brain is adjusting to being awake. Sometimes you can't get there... you have to go back to bed and sleep after getting up just an hour or two earlier.

You have a sense of great loss. You are not the same. For so many reasons, the essence of who you are is gone. You don't do what you used to do like work or drive or be with friends. You almost don't care sometimes because it's all you can do to think about getting through the day with the chaos that is now part of your world.

You feel fragile, broken. You feel damaged. How do you pick up all the pieces and make progress?

You think "what has happened?", "did this really happen to me?", "is this all my life is going to be like?" "am I ever going to get better?", "it's been 6 months and I'm still not better", "this is terrible, but I have to be grateful it's not worse and that I'm alive".

It goes on and on and on for months, for years but gradually you get better. You make progress but it is very slow. It takes years. Sometimes you encounter relapses. Sometimes you have symptoms you thought were gone but they are back because you are stressed or tired or over-stimulated or sick.

Someone very close to me recently asked me about my brain injury recovery and said, "When did it all end?" I said, "It didn't end". It never ends. It's always there sometimes better, sometimes worse. There are more days now where I don't think about it because I do quite well. I am grateful for the progress I've made and most people who didn't know me before wouldn't know the difference. But I know. I remember how I used to be. I haven't gotten it all back but I'm still working on it. Like so many of you with brain injuries, I realize how strong I have been to have gotten through all this and I am grateful I am doing as well as I am. I am proud of myself and the hard work I've put into my recovery. I'm sure many of you feel the same way.

Source: thebrainfairy.com (Permission received

Part of my mental therapy was in writing this book. It was a way to sort my thoughts, piece together the lost pieces of this journey, and to also give advice and reinforcement to my fellow nurses. Hence, "Nursing From The Other Side." It gives the point of view of a nurse being a patient, and hopefully gives insight to the profession of nursing, and to those who have faced or will face a catastrophic illness. Never stop learning or caring. So, to my fellow nurses/caregivers, always remember this:

1. Have passion for what you do; love being a nurse.

2. Listen to your patients; hear what they are saying.

3. Spend time with your patients; be at the bedside.

4. Learn to prioritize your time. It is your responsibility.

5. Your patients expect to be cared for, have someone they can trust; they deserve the best you can give. Live up to their expectations.

As for me, in my heart I will always be a nurse, and for now I will just have to be a voice for the nurse/patient. Each day I will face the challenges presented to me; facing every challenge, "One day at a time…"

SUGGESTED RESOURCES

Websites

www.stroke.org

www.flintrehab.com

www.brainaneurysmfoundation

www.pubmed.gov/Medline

www.socialsecurity.gov/disability

www.thebrainfairy.com

- Contact your local agency on aging

- Search the internet and social media for information

Support groups on Facebook

Stroke Support group with Flint Rehab

Brain Aneurysm/AVM Support Group by the Joe Niekro Foundation

- Many local communities have support groups; ask your neurosurgeon

Books

- HAPPINESS AND HEALING AFTER STROKE: by Kari Dahlgren
- STRONGER AFTER STROKE: by Peter G. Levine
- THE BRAIN'S WAY OF HEALING: by Norman Doidge, MD
- NEUROPLASTICITY: by Eric Smith